REMARKABLE KIND OF *Love*

PASTOR WILBERT WATSON

Copyright © 2024 Pastor Wilbert Watson.

All rights reserved. No part of this book may be reproduced, stored, or transmitted by any means—whether auditory, graphic, mechanical, or electronic—without written permission of both publisher and author, except in the case of brief excerpts used in critical articles and reviews. Unauthorized reproduction of any part of this work is illegal and is punishable by law.

ISBN: 979-8-89419-334-2 (sc)
ISBN: 979-8-89419-335-9 (hc)
ISBN: 979-8-89419-336-6 (e)

Because of the dynamic nature of the Internet, any web addresses or links contained in this book may have changed since publication and may no longer be valid. The views expressed in this work are solely those of the author and do not necessarily reflect the views of the publisher, and the publisher hereby disclaims any responsibility for them.

One Galleria Blvd., Suite 1900, Metairie, LA 70001
(504) 702-6708

CONTENTS

Description v

Preface vii

Chapter 1   God Loves Never Fades or Fails 1

Chapter 2   Love is the Greatest 5

Chapter 3   Don't Follow the Crowd and Miss Out 12

Chapter 4   Listen for The Holy Spirit's Guidance 19

Chapter 5   Go and Make Disciples 24

Chapter 6   Say The Right Thing at The Right Time 31

Chapter 7   You Must Know the Word for Yourself 37

Chapter 8   Time for God's People to Recommit 41

Chapter 9   Remember Where Our True Home Is 46

Chapter 10 The Old Has Gone The New is Here 53

Chapter 11 Which Life Do You Want? 58

Chapter 12 Show GOD, You Love Him! 64

DESCRIPTION

This fourth book of Pastor Wilbert Watson, is to encourage many world-wide to know for sure that God's love is definitely genuine and unconditional. Furthermore, encourage as many as possible, to pursue a strong consistent personal relationship with God. One of the most well-known scriptures in the Bible, is John 3:16; it summarizes the sacrificial nature of God's love. It also shows how God willingly gave His only begotten Son to guarantee salvation of humanity; that's love! But salvation is a choice that human make; Jesus is the only way, and the only one who can give salvation. He was chosen by God to be our Savior, not man! Salvation is God's grace! God's nature is love and remarkable but many still have a hard time comprehending God's love for them. It's important that everyone understand that God wants all of us to love Him wholeheartedly in every way possible. We can show God how much we love Him by having a personal relationship with Him and making sure we spend quality time with Him. When God is first priority in our lives; we will make sure He gets the quality time before anybody or anything. We cannot just talk about putting God first, we must apply His godly principles every day.

PREFACE

The purpose of this book spread the remarkable unconditional love of God worldwide. This book will help many to understand and appreciate the deepness and freedom of God's love that changes everything. God sent His only Son to die for our sins, showing us a love that we as believers and followers of Jesus Christ are called to show to others as well. Even in our relationship with others.

> 1 John 4:7-12 (ESV), states, *"7Beloved, let us love one another, for love is from God, and whoever loves has been born of God and knows God. 8Anyone who does not love does not know God, because God is love. 9In this the love of God was made manifest among us, that God sent his only Son into the world, so that we might live through him. 10In this is love, not that we have loved God but that he loved us and sent his Son to be the propitiation for our sins. 11Beloved, if God so loved us, we also ought to love one another. 12No one has ever seen God; if we love one another, God abides in us and his love is perfected in us."*

True godly love in a person's life is a clear indication or sign of being born again. Those who truly love God will show true remarkable unconditional love to other people.

Chapter 1

GOD LOVES NEVER FADES OR FAILS

Glory and honor to God; His love, never fades or fails! It's important that we all know, God loves us, with a love that never fades. God's love is unwavering or steadfast; human love, is often subject to change. God's love will not fall or falter; His love is constant forever.

> Isaiah 43:4 (NIV), says, *"Since you are precious and honored in my sight, and because I love you, I will give people in exchange for you, nations in exchange for your life."*

God loves and values His people, He will give-up men and nations for them in exchange for their lives. Yes, this is part of a prophesy of deliverance and redemption from Egypt. But God's perfect love never fades or fails, it only goes deeper and deeper every day. You and others need to know we are surrounded by God's love, every day. I've realized there will be times that can lead us to ask: "if I can still experience the same miracles and blessings as others? God's love surrounds us but is not always felt; it's because our heart longs for something different than what is already there. You could be covered or distracted by too much noise that you forget God's voice. But no matter where life will take you, know that God's love never fades, fails or leaves you.

Anything in this life will fade, anyone in your life, will be gone, but God's love remains, and it only goes deeper every single day. You are more loved than you know! Your actual worth is not of this world but Him who created you. Although you cannot avoid thinking, doubting and fearing things or people; but remember; your thoughts will remain as thoughts unless they happen. There is a huge difference between overthinking and thinking wisely. Overthinking involves thinking about a certain topic or situation excessively, analyzing it for long periods of time. When we overthink, we have a hard time getting our mind to focus on anything else. It becomes consumed by the one thing we are thinking about.

Wise people realize that they are always in control of their thoughts, feelings, and actions. Most people let others' behavior affect them negatively. As a result, they let that negativity infiltrate or fill their lives and make them miserable. Instead, let their bad behavior roll-off your shoulders. Yeap! Let their bad behavior just roll-off your shoulders. God will teach you how to think the way He wants for you. That's why it is important to fill your thoughts, first thing every single day, with God's promises and words. You must constantly remind yourself that you want to swim in God's love and not drown by the standards of this world.

How can we keep our mind focused on God when we have so many distractions or disruptions in our daily lives? Start each day saying, I'm going to stay close to Jesus Christ; don't get so caught-up in your work or other daily activities that you barely give God a thought, the rest of the day. It's important to remember that even when we forget God; He never forgets us. God knows what's happening to us every moment of the day, and He also watches over us. The reason is because He loves us with a love that never fades or fails.

Read this part in Isaiah 43:4 again: "You are precious and honored in my sight, and I love you." God does want us to walk with Him every moment of the day and the first step is to begin the day with Him. Mornings are rushed or hurried for most of us but develop the habit of setting aside a few minutes to be alone with God. Pray about things you know you'll be facing that day, and read a portion of God's Word, the Bible. Then let that portion of the Bible take root in your soul all day long, remembering it and calling it to mind.

In addition, develop the habit of constant prayer. When you meet someone new, say a silent prayer for them. When you learn about a problem someone is having; pray for them. When someone tries your patience, pray for them. First Thessalonians 5:17, says, *"Pray continually"*

Ask God to remind you of His love for you not just at church once a week or at the end of the day, but repeatedly. Someday, we will be in Christ's presence forever but may it, begin now.

In conclusion, according to God's word, we are precious in His sight. It is very clear that we are precious to God because we are His creation. Our lives and our deaths are matters of deep concern for God. Scripture reveals God's eternal love for us, a love that never fails. As a matter of fact, nothing at all can separate us from God's eternal love. God's love is sacrificial and unconditional; it is overwhelming and welcoming! God unconditional love for each of us runs so deep that we are called children of God. Because of God's love; we are His children. There is no reason to be afraid when you realize what God has done for you. God promises to be with us; He will take us through the fire! At the exodus, He took Israel through the red sea and defeated the Egyptian army. Perhaps the three Hebrew heroes claimed this promise, when they faced the fiery furnace. I know God has watched over and protected me from birth; my God is my protection, and with Him, I am safe!

Glory to God!!!

NOTES:

Chapter 2

LOVE IS THE GREATEST

On Christmas Eve and Christmas day; like many, at our church, Divine Faith Ministry, in Petersburg, Virginia, like many worldwide, we celebrate God's love through the birth of His Son, Jesus Christ. Jesus is the Son of God who came to earth as a human baby and grew-up to die on a cross for the sins of humanity. Jesus' birth was prophesied or foretold by the prophets and recorded in the Bible. Christmas is a time of spiritual reflection and joy for Christians who believe in Jesus as their Savior, and Lord. The true meaning of Christmas is clearly expressed, in John 3:16-17:

> *"For God so loved the world that he gave his one and only Son, that whoever believes in him shall not perish but have eternal life. For God did not send his Son into the world to condemn the world, but to save the world through him."*

But why did God do such a thing? He did such a thing because He loves us; love is the greatest!

_____

_____

_____

_____

First Corinthians 13 (NKJV), says: *¹Though I speak with the tongues of men and of angels, but have not love, I have become sounding brass or a clanging cymbal. ²And though I have the gift of prophecy, and understand all mysteries and all knowledge, and though I have all faith, so that I could remove mountains, but have not love, I am nothing. ³And though I bestow all my goods to feed the poor, and though I give my body [a]to be burned, but have not love, it profits me nothing. ⁴Love suffers long and is kind; love does not envy; love does not parade itself, is not [b]puffed up; ⁵does not behave rudely, does not seek its own, is not provoked, [c]thinks no evil; ⁶does not rejoice in iniquity, but rejoices in the truth; ⁷bears all things, believes all things, hopes all things, endures all things. ⁸Love never fails. But whether there are prophecies, they will fail; whether there are tongues, they will cease; whether there is knowledge, it will vanish away. ⁹For we know in part and we prophesy in part. ¹⁰But when that which is [d]perfect has come, then that which is in part will be done away. ¹¹When I was a child, I spoke as a child, I understood as a child, I thought as a child; but when I became a man, I put away childish things. ¹²For now we see in a mirror, dimly, but then face to face. Now I know in part, but then I shall know just as I also am known. ¹³And now abide faith, hope, love, these three; but the greatest of these is love."*

_____

_____

_____

_____

The whole 1 Corinthians Chapter 13, is thoroughly or popular because the entire book revolves around **LOVE.** The greatest gift we can ever give and receive, is love; it is the greatest because God showed us through His Son, Jesus Christ**,** how great His love is for us. I am expressing the indescribable gift that God gave us human beings through His Son, Jesus Christ because of his love for us. Through that expression from God; we know that "love is the greatest. Love is everlasting and never-ending; the greatest expression of God's love for us is described or written in John 3:16:

> *"For God so loved the world that he gave his one and only Son, that whoever believes in him shall not perish but have eternal (everlasting) life."*

John 3:16 has been called a "love letter" from God, written in blood and addressed to everyone. If ever there was a verse that Satan would love to blot-out or erase from the Bible, it would be, John 3:16. If ever there was a verse that makes hell tremble, it is John 3:16. If ever there was a verse that has lightened the path to heaven for multitudes, it is John 3:16.

First Corinthians 13 is the apostle Paul's first letter to the church of Corinth to challenge believers to examine their lives against the image (or likeness) of Jesus Christ. Above all the apostle Paul especially placed a lot of emphasis on "love," Jesus Christ's love. Apostle Paul's mission was to unify the church and bring them together in fellowship. First Corinthians 13, truly expresses that love is the most important thing for Christians to have and practice in their daily lives. It furthermore teaches us; without love, the spiritual gifts are worthless. And describes the nature of love, which is patient, kind, humble, and enduring. It compares or contrasts love with the gifts which are temporary and will pass away, while love is eternal (love is everlasting).

We are encouraged as Christians to imitate the love of Jesus and serve others with love. God's love is totally unconditional; He demonstrates His unconditional love for each of us by providing a way for every person to be made right. God is not like human beings; He does not pick and chooses who He loves. He loves all of us! God's love for us is unconditional and it cannot be increased or decreased by anything we do. There is nothing you or anyone else can do, to make God love us less. There is nothing you or anyone else can do to make God love us more. However, God's love for everyone does not mean that everyone will be saved (see Matthew 25:46).

God will not ignore sin, for He is a God of justice (2 Thessalonians 1:6). Sin cannot go unpunished forever (Romans 3:25–26). If God simply disregarded sin and allowed it to continue to wreak havoc in creation forever, then He would not be love. To ignore God's merciful love, to reject Christ, or to deny the Savior who bought us (2 Peter 2:1) is to subject ourselves to God's wrath for eternity (Romans 1:18), not His love. Love is the greatest gift because it is life's greatest gift. It's more important than spiritual gifts, preaching, knowledge, and faith. Love defines us, creates bonds, gives strength, and builds our faith. It is part of the oneness of life and we can feel its presence, if we open our senses and hearts. Love is the way we love as God loves, even when others don't deserve it.

Jesus is the Savior who delivers us from sin and death (Matthew 1:21). He is the human Messiah (Christ) who fulfills the Law (Matthew 5:17). Jesus is the divine Lord who has entered our world: the Almighty has taken on human flesh; God and man have been fused or united together in an indivisible (inseparable), eternal bond; God is truly with us.

I would be remiss, if I did not mention that 1 Corinthians 13 (the love chapter), is often read at weddings. It's often read at weddings because it beautifully captures the essence or the heart of love. It speaks to the idea that love is not just a fleeting or fading emotion, or a superficial feeling, but rather a deep and selfless commitment. The verses in 1 Corinthians Chapter 13 describe love as patient and kind; not envious or boastful. It emphasizes the importance of putting others before ourselves and not seeking our own interests. Love is described as not being easily angered and keeping no record of wrongs. It is a forgiving and compassionate love that seeks reconciliation and understanding. These verses in 1 Corinthians 13, also highlight the enduring or long-term nature of love. It says that love never fails, even when other things like prophecies or knowledge may cease.

_____

_____

_____

_____

Love is eternal and everlasting; it is the foundation upon which relationships are built and sustained. When these verses are read at weddings, they serve as a reminder to the couple and those in attendance of the true meaning and purpose of love. It is not just about the excitement and passion of the wedding day, but about the commitment to love and cherish one another in sickness and in health, for better or for worse. I share this about First Corinthians 13 because it's not limited to romantic love, but can be applied to all forms of love. It speaks to the importance of love in our relationships with family, friends, and even strangers.

Love is the driving force behind acts of kindness, forgiveness, and selflessness.

First Corinthians 13 is read at weddings because it beautifully articulates or expresses the qualities and purpose of love. It serves as a reminder to the couple and those in attendance to prioritize love in their relationships, and to always strive to embody or exemplify the characteristics of love described in the verses of 1 Corinthians 13. Love is the greatest because God is love, every Christian must model God's love. How that is to be done is described in 1 Corinthians 13; keeping in mind that God's love is an expression of His essence or spirit. The essence of every Christian must express itself, in love.

Love is greater than faith and hope in that both faith and hope depend on love for their existence. Without love, there can be no true faith; a loveless faith is nothing but an empty religious exercise. As apostle Paul says, "If I have a faith that can move mountains, but do not have love, I am nothing" (1 Corinthians 13:2). Without love, there can be no genuine hope; a loveless hope is an oxymoron, or just a figure of speech. Because we cannot truly hope for something that we do not love. Faith and hope are dead sterile things if not accompanied by love.

In conclusion, God does not just love; He **is love.** His nature and essence, are love. God is love! He created love, created us to love Him, and has extended His love to each of us. Our challenge is to accept His great love

(Ephesians 2:8-9) that we may experience His love in our lives today and for eternity (John 3:16). The fullest expression of God as love was through the Son, Jesus Christ. God does not only give love; He is the source of love. As the Creator of all things (Genesis 1:1) He is the One who created love. It is because of His love that we are able to love. As 1 John 4:19 notes, *"We love because he first loved us.* Whoever does not love does not know God, because God is love."

The one who does not love has not become acquainted with God; because God is love! Jesus gave us the first and greatest commandment in Matthew 22:36–40:

> *"Love the Lord your God with all your heart, soul, mind, and strength."*

NOTES:

Chapter 3

DON'T FOLLOW THE CROWD AND MISS OUT

Don't follow the crowd and miss out; without a doubt; others can affect or impact our behavior or conduct. One reason for this; we live in a very difficult or complicated world. We use the decisions of others as an experimental, or mental shortcut to navigate our lives. We don't accept Jesus Christ for others; we do it, for ourself. We are responsible for our own salvation. When the desire of someone else replaces or take the place of the desire of God; we have fallen or slipped into idolatry (Exodus 20:3; 34:14). Love for the world pushes out love for God, and love for God pushes out love for the world.

> As Jesus said in Matthew 6:24, *"No one can serve two masters; for either he will hate the one and love the other, or he will be devoted to the one and despise the other. You cannot serve God and money."*

This chapter is to encourage you and many others to not follow the crowd. Don't follow the crowd in doing wrong; the most important person we are to follow is Jesus Christ. Everyone follows something: friends, popular culture, family, selfish desires, or God. We can only follow one thing at a time (Matthew 6:24). God says, in his Word, we are to have no other gods before Him. To truly follow Christ means we do not follow anything else;

it's important to stay true to yourself. Don't follow the crowd, and miss out. Many people will choose a path that most people travel, rather than a path, people less travel. We should not allow ourselves to be pushed or pressured into following the corrupt customs, ungodly principles, or evil plans of action promoted by worldly people. The blessed man, according to Psalm 1:1 (NKJV), resists being conformed to the pattern of the world:

> *"Blessed is the man Who walks not in the counsel of the ungodly, Nor stands in the path of sinners, Nor sits in the seat of the scornful;*
>
> Luke 13:24, says, *"Strive to enter through the narrow gate, for many, I tell you, will attempt to enter but will not be strong enough."*

There are really, only two roads we can travel in this life: one, the wide road or two, the narrow road. The wide road is every other religious or spiritual belief outside of true Christianity. It is well-traveled but leads to destruction. God's word says, *"Enter by the narrow gate; For wide is the gate and broad is the way that leads to destruction, and many enter through it"* (Matthew 7:13; NKJV). The narrow road is a genuine or true personal relationship and trust in Christ Jesus; it's the only road that leads to life. Follow Jesus, to enter heaven. I want to encourage you in accordance with God's Word to make sure you are on the right road or path. Every one of us, must decide which spiritual path is the right path, and walk it; walk it, and live it!

> Matthew 7: 21-23, says, *"Not everyone who says to Me, 'Lord, Lord,' shall enter the kingdom of heaven, but he who does the will of My Father in heaven. Many will say to Me in that day, 'Lord, Lord, have we not prophesied in Your name, cast out demons in Your name, and done many wonders in Your name?' And then I will declare to them, 'I never knew you; depart from Me, you who practice lawlessness!"*

If you recalled previously reading Luke 13:24; it really shows or confirms that we cannot enter Heaven by our own will, or through our own effort.

Furthermore, it warns us though some will try to get to Heaven through their own effort; this approach will not work. Upon meeting our Lord; after death, they will be surprised that they are not a member of God's Kingdom. Jesus came to seek and save the lost, but unfortunately, not all of the lost want to be found. The unfortunate reality of the narrow and wide gates Jesus spoke of is not all of us, will choose correctly. Many will follow the mainstream or the crowd, and miss out on an eternal life opportunity in heaven. The narrow gate, also called the narrow door is referred to by the Lord Jesus in Matthew 7:13-14 and Luke 13:23-24. Jesus compares the narrow gate to the "broad road" which leads to destruction (hell) and says that "many" will be on that road. By contrast or comparison, Jesus says that "small is the gate and narrow the road that leads to life, and only a few find it."

What exactly is meant by this? Just how many are the "many" and how few are the "few?" First of all; we need to truly understand that Jesus is the Door through which all must enter eternal life. There is no other way because He alone is "the way, the truth and the life" (John 14:6). The Bible teaches that there is no other way to salvation than through Jesus Christ. Jesus Himself says in John 14:6, *"I am the way, the truth, and the life. No one comes to the Father except through me."*

The way to eternal life is restricted to just one avenue or one way; Jesus Christ! In this sense, the way is narrow because it is the only way, and relatively few people will go through, the narrow gate. Many more will attempt to find another route or way to God. They will try to get there through man-made rules and regulations, through false religion, or through self-effort. John 10:7-11, tells us; *"These who are "many" will follow the broad road that leads to eternal destruction, while the sheep hear the voice of the Good Shepherd and follow Him along the narrow way to eternal life."*

Sadly, there are many false believers who will be expecting to go to Heaven, and will be denied entrance. The best way to avoid being one is to make sure; you have truly put your trust in Jesus Christ, alone for salvation. Many people follow false teachings from the Bible given by false preachers, or they just refuse to obey instructions from God, and follow their own minds. There are many people who throw on the Christian name tag, and they think by just going to church, they will be granted Heaven, which is false.

> Isaiah 29:13, reads, *"And so the Lord says, These people say they are mine. They honor me with their lips, but their hearts are far from me. And their worship of me is nothing but man-made rules learned by rote (learned by repetition or habit)."*

Just like there are fake or counterfeit $20, $50-, AND $100-DOLLAR bills; it's no surprise that there are also fake or phony Christians, within the body of Christ. Jesus Himself, spoke about this when He gave the parable of the wheat and the tares. In Matthew 13:24-30, You may remember or recalled how Jesus said that there was a farmer who sowed good seed in his field.

At night, his enemy went and sowed weeds among his good seeds. So, when the crops began to grow, so did the weeds. So, the farmer's workers asked the farmer, "Sir, the land that you planted, is filled with weeds. Where did they come from?" So, the farmer replied, "An enemy planted these weeds." So, the workers asked, "Do you want us to go into the field and take out the weeds?" But the farmer surprised his workers by saying, "No, you'll uproot the wheat if you do that. Let both grow together until the time of the harvest. Then I will tell the harvesters to sort out the weeds, tie them into bundles, and burn them. And I'll tell the harvesters to put the wheat in my barn."

That's why it's important for you to be able to spot fake or phony Christians because you'll want to include them in your evangelism efforts. Just Keeping it real with you! When you received Christ; the Holy Spirit came and began living inside of you. Walking in the flesh instead of the Spirit can be an indication or sign that something fishy or shady is going on (Galatians 5:16-18). When we were born again, we became a new creation with new desires, a new mind, and new heart. If there isn't evidence of any of these: a new creation with new desires, a new mind, and new heart. This is a serious problem, and can hinder your travel on the right path. The fruit of the Spirit is love, joy, peace, longsuffering, kindness, goodness, faithfulness, gentleness, and self-control (Galatians 5:22- 23). Genuine Christians will have these spiritual fruits, in their lives.

Strive to enter through the narrow gate; man will attempt to enter but will not be strong enough. We can enter God's Kingdom only through the narrow gate. The highway to hell is broad, and its gate is wide for the many, who choose that way. But the gateway to life is very narrow and the road is difficult, and only a few ever find it. One of the meanings of the word "find" is *"To come upon or discover by searching or making an effort."* To find something, requires some effort from the person who is searching for it. The gate and the way represent the same thing. The broad way has a wide gate and the narrow way has a narrow gate. The message from our Lord and Savior, Jesus Christ, should have the effect of causing us to honestly step-back and look at our own life to sincerely and humbly, examine the path, that we are on. Jesus' straightforwardness or caution and clarity on this real experience that some will have; should help to open their eyes to honestly examine if Jesus is speaking about him or her. It takes true humility to face the truth, at times, and to admit if we are trying to rely more upon ourselves, than upon Christ. The "narrow gate" is that gate through which the humble enter. Pride and self-sufficiency lead us to attempt to make our own path to Heaven. But this path is never the correct one.

In conclusion, entering the "narrow gate" also means that we listen to God. He as the divine Shepherd and always calling to us in a gentle way. Only when we are attentive to His voice, will we know where He is leading us. Only then will we discover the way through the one and only narrow gate. Today, reflect or think about, upon that moment when you meet our Lord face-to-face. What will that encounter be like? Will it be one where Jesus greets you with open arms saying: *"WELL, done, good and faithful servant, enter into your reward."* Or will it be one in which He says, "I do not know you." Now is the time to face your life of faith with honesty, striving to rely only upon the strength of our divine Lord. Don't follow the crowd and miss out on your eternal life in heaven, with Jesus Christ. God is just and he denies no one a genuine chance at salvation. God has given us the free gift of eternal life with Him. Opportunity is an appropriate time to act; it is a moment of time in your life that, when maximized, will define and impact your life and destiny. Every turning point in life; is a result of opportunity you make effective use of.

Glory to God!

NOTES:

Chapter 4

LISTEN FOR THE HOLY SPIRIT'S GUIDANCE

Before Jesus ascended to heaven, He told His disciples that He would send one who would teach and **guide** all those who believe in Him (Acts 1:5; John 14:26; 16:7). Jesus' promise was fulfilled less than two weeks later when the Holy Spirit came in power on the believers at Pentecost (Acts 2). Now, when a person believes in Christ, the Holy Spirit immediately, or instantly becomes a permanent part of his or her life (Romans 8:14; 1 Corinthians 12:13; Ephesians 1:13–14). The Holy Spirit has many functions. Not only does He distribute spiritual gifts according to His will (1 Corinthians 12:7–11), but He also comforts us (John 14:16, KJV), and teaches us (John 14:26), and remains in us as a seal of promise upon our hearts until the day of Jesus' return (Ephesians 1:13; 4:30). The Holy Spirit also takes on the role of Guide, and Counselor, leading us in the way we should go and revealing God's truth (Luke 12:12; 1 Corinthians 2:6–10).

Listen for the Holy Spirit's guidance; in John 14:26: Jesus describes the Holy Spirit.

> *"But the Advocate, the Holy Spirit, whom the Father will send in my name, will teach you all things and will remind you of everything I have said to you."*

If we listen for the Holy Spirit's guidance, it will be easier to know what's right. Jesus glorifies the Father (God). He does it through His people as they do God's work and keeps His commandments. Apart from the power of the Holy Spirit and prayer, we could never glorify the Lord. It's one thing for us to go to heaven and quite something else for heaven to come to us. There is a deeper fellowship with the Son (Jesus Christ), and the Father for those who love Him, seek Him, and obey Him. We experience His peace and presence as we, commune with the Father and the Son, in love. Jesus, is the way to the Father; He reveals the truth about the Father; and He shares the life of the father with us.

So, why should our hearts be troubled? If a believer truly loves and obeys the Lord, he or she will experience fellowship with God. If a person does not love God; he or she will not, obey him. Keeping it real with you! God wants a person heart, not lip service! God is not impressed with lip service; we must worship God in spirit and truth. disobedience is a serious matter; Jesus' words, are the words of God.

Jesus told his disciples these things while he was with them, but the holy spirit came, he would remind the disciples of all things that Jesus had said, and would teach all things (see 1 Corinthians 2:13):

> *"This is what we speak, not in words taught us by human wisdom but in words taught by the Spirit, explaining spiritual realities with Spirit-taught words."*

This promise was primarily fulfilled through the lives of the apostles in the writing of the New Testament. Matthew and John wrote down Jesus' words. Peter wrote about the gospel in his two letters and may have dictated some of the memories of Jesus to mark. In 1 Corinthians 2:13, the apostle Paul emphasized that the intellectuals of this world could not teach the knowledge he was giving to the Corinthian believers. Notice the spirit did not simply dictate words to Paul and the other apostles; he taught them. The apostles related with their own vocabulary and style what they had learn from the spirit.

But how do we recognize the holy spirit guidance? How do we discern between our own thoughts and His leading? After all, the Holy Spirit does not speak with audible words. He guides us through our own consciences (Romans 9:1), and other quiet, subtle ways. One of the most important ways to recognize the Holy Spirit's guidance is to be familiar with God's Word. The Bible is the ultimate source of wisdom about how we should live (2 Timothy 3:16), and believers are to search the Scriptures, meditate on them, and commit them to memory (Joshua 1:8). The Word is the "sword of the Spirit" (Ephesians 6:17), and the Spirit will use it to speak to us (John 16:12–14), to reveal God's will for our lives; He will also bring specific Scriptures to mind at times when we need them most (John 14:26).

Knowledge of God's Word can help us to discern whether or not our desires come from the Holy Spirit.

We must test our inclinations or our learnings against Scripture; the Holy Spirit will never prod or poke us to do anything contrary or conflicting to God's Word. If it conflicts with the Bible, then it is not from the Holy Spirit, and should be ignored. Once again, if it conflicts with the Bible, then it is not from the Holy Spirit and should be ignored. It is also necessary for us to be in continual prayer with the Father (1 Thessalonians 5:17). Not only does this keep our hearts and minds open to the Holy Spirit's leading, but it also allows the Spirit to speak on our behalf:

> Romans 8:26–27, says, *"In the same way, the Spirit helps us in our weakness. We do not know what we ought to pray for, but the Spirit himself intercedes for us through wordless groans. And he who searches our hearts knows the mind of the Spirit, because the Spirit intercedes for God's people in accordance with the will of God"*

Another way to tell if we are following the Spirit's leading is to look for signs of His fruit in our lives (Galatians 5:22–23). If we walk in the Spirit, we will continue to see these qualities grow and mature in us, and they will become evident to others as well.

It's important to note that we have the choice whether or not to accept the Holy Spirit's guidance. When we know the will of God, but do not follow it, we are resisting the Spirit's work in our lives (Acts 7:51; 1 Thessalonians 5:19), and a desire to follow our own way grieves Him (Ephesians 4:30). The Holy Spirit will never lead us into sin. Habitual sin will cause us to miss what the Holy Spirit wants to say to us through the Word. Being in tune with God's will, turning from and confessing sin, and making a habit of prayer and the study of God's Word, will allow us to recognize, and follow the holy Spirit's leading.

I wrote earlier, Jesus describes the Holy Spirit in John 14:26):

> *"But the Advocate, the Holy Spirit, whom the Father will send in my name, will teach you all things and will remind you of everything I have said to you."*

Jesus is our Advocate with the Father; our Lord and Savior, Jesus Christ is the bridge between us and God. Glory to God! Thank God for His indescribable gift! Jesus is our Advocate, our Lord. He advocates for us; He intercedes for us; and He stands in our place. We don't get what we deserve; instead, we get grace after grace, God's Mercy, and God's unfailing, unconditional and everlasting love. The blood of Jesus, speaks for me and you, but one of the questions people ask the most is: "How do I hear the Holy Spirit?" They think there must be a magic formula involved, and while there is not a 1-2-3 magic formula; there are disciplines that you can implement to put yourself in the place of hearing the Holy Spirit more clearly. Remember, the Holy Spirit is always speaking; it's just a matter of us opening our spiritual ears to hear Him.

In conclusion, how we hear the Holy Spirit; listen. The Holy Spirit is talking; it's up to us to hear Him clearly. We can improve our ability to hear the Holy Spirit by focusing more on God's Word, listening to genuine Holy Spirit-filled people of God, and in prayer. You will improve your ability to hear the Holy Spirit, and you will have the joy of living a Spirit-led life! Listen for the Holy Spirit's guidance; the Holy Spirit will speak to your heart. Trust me, the Holy Spirit will not contradict the Bible.

NOTES:

Chapter 5

GO AND MAKE DISCIPLES

Matthew 28:16-20 (NIV), says, *"16 Then the eleven disciples went to Galilee, to the mountain where Jesus had told them to go. 17 When they saw him, they worshiped him; but some doubted. 18 Then Jesus came to them and said, "All authority in heaven and on earth has been given to me. 19 Therefore go and make disciples of all nations, baptizing them in the name of the Father and of the Son and of the Holy Spirit, 20 and teaching them to obey everything I have commanded you. And SURELY, I am with you always, to the very end of the age."*

The Great Commission was not just for the immediate disciples that Jesus was speaking to, but it is given to all believers. Today, the Great Commission is still being fulfilled by international missionary work, by local churches in actively seeking the lost, in their community, in outreach activities, and by believers witnessing for Jesus Christ to their NEXT-DOOR neighbor. The Great Commission spells-out the main purpose of all believers. After salvation or deliverance, our lives belong to Jesus Christ who died to purchase our freedom from sin and death.

Jesus redeemed us (paid the price for us) so that we might become useful in his Kingdom. It's important that we know what "The Great Commission" means and is; half of U.S. churchgoers (51 percent) say they do not know this term: "The Great Commission." One in four (25 percent), said they had heard the term but weren't sure, what it meant. Sadly, just 17 percent said they knew "the Great Commission" is Jesus assigning His followers to spread the Gospel. It is important that everyone who reads chapter 5 in this book truly understand exactly what The Great Commission is and the significance of it.

The Great Commission is and why Jesus' Great Commission is still important today. After Jesus Christ's death on the cross, He was buried and then resurrected on the third day. Before He ascended into heaven, He appeared to his disciples in Galilee and gave them these instructions in Matthew 28:

> *"[18] Then Jesus came to them and said, "All authority in heaven and on earth has been given to me. [19] Therefore go and make disciples of all nations, baptizing them in the name of the Father and of the Son and of the Holy Spirit, [20] and teaching them to obey everything I have commanded you. And SURELY, I am with you always, to the very end of the age."*

Go and make disciples is a command from Jesus to His followers to spread His teachings to all nations (all people). It is also known as "The Great Commission," to put your faith into action and Go Make Disciples. We as Christians or believers must move to where people are, use what they have, teach what Jesus taught, invite others to go with them, and trust the Holy Spirit to work.

The Catholic Church in the United States has a national plan and strategy for evangelization, based on this command: "Go and make disciples!" The Great Commission spells out the main purpose of all believers. After salvation, our lives belong to Jesus Christ who died to purchase our freedom from sin and death. He redeemed us so that we might become useful in His Kingdom. Fulfillment of the "Great Commission" happens when believers witness or share their testimony (Acts 1:8):

Preach the gospel (Mark 16:15), baptize new converts, and teach the Word of God (Matthew 28:20). Christians are to replicate themselves (make disciples) in the lives of those who respond to the message of Christ's salvation. Christians do not have to strive to fulfill the Great Commission.

The Holy Spirit is the One who empowers believers to carry out the Great Commission and the One who convicts people of their need for a Savior (John 16:8–11). The success of the mission depends on Jesus Christ, who promised to always be with His disciples as they carry-out their assignment (Matthew 28:20). Both His presence and His authority will accompany us to accomplish His disciple-making mission. The full text of the most familiar version of The Great Commission is recorded in Matthew 28:16-20. But it is also found in each of the Gospel texts (Matthew, Mark, Luke and John).

Although each version varies; these passages record an encounter of Jesus with his disciples after the resurrection. In each instance, Jesus sends His followers out with specific instructions. He uses commands such as "go, teach, baptize, forgive, and make."

Why The Great Commission meaning and importance in this book?
Because God cares about the souls of His image bearers and so must we. Our friends, family, coworkers, neighbors, and acquaintances who do not know Jesus Christ will endure God's wrath forever, if they do not trust Jesus before they die. So, we as believers, have the responsibility for our children in our homes, but the church is responsible for "the great commission." And the "Great Commission" teaches us to make disciples. We are responsible to make disciples of the present and next generation. **Glory to God!**

The main way Jesus began the biggest movement in human history (Christianity) was by calling, developing, and sending out a handful of unqualified, untrained, and unlikely disciples. It was common in the first century for a Jewish rabbi (scholar or leader) to have, and lead disciples, who were pupils or students that were so devoted to their leader that they accepted their teaching and adhered to their lifestyle. They not only learned information, but they walked with their teacher in order to become like them. More than that, true disciples assisted their leaders in spreading their mission.

One major sign of maturity in a disciple is a willingness to help *others follow;* that's why Jesus stood on a hillside in Galilee, at the end of His ministry, and gave His disciples His final command to "Go therefore and make disciples of all nations" (Matthew 28:19). This commission is so "Great" because of its timeless importance to Christianity and the fact that all the gospel writers included similar versions of it (Mark 16; Luke 24:44-49; John 21; Acts 1:6-8).

What did Jesus mean when He said to "Go and make disciples?"
Jesus was instructing His faithful followers to leave where they were, go find others, and invite them to follow Him, too. But the deeper question is on "how" Jesus wanted them to do it? Thankfully, Jesus answered this question when He explained, throughout each of the Great Commission passages: to teach what he taught, be witnesses of his life, preach repentance and the forgiveness of sin, "feed" the "sheep," and baptize in His name.

When Jesus gave this Great Commission, we can know that He gave it with all power, enabling believers to live out the message of the Gospel in a way that is entirely subject to He who has made salvation possible. The mission cannot fail because the authority of Christ cannot fail. This is hope-spurning to every believer who participates in the Great Commission. We are invited to join in on doing the victorious work which only God can do: that is making disciples for the One who holds all authority.

The Great Commission Matters Because Of What Jesus said: Jesus was not suggesting how believers could live, He was giving a command. The life of Jesus was an example of how to make disciples of every nation, and it was time for all those who had learned from Him, to follow in His footsteps. We must look at these words and remember that Jesus was not simply commanding world-evangelism, but He was commanding that disciple be made. To make a disciple is to teach a Christian what their new identity in Christ means, and how they are to live in it!

Jesus made disciples by years of teaching His followers how to live in Him. There are two parts to this, which Jesus tells believers to lead others into:

(1) public proclamation of faith, baptism, and
(2) teaching the new believers all that He taught.

This is for every nation, every tribe, every tongue, every individual. There is not one person whom the Lord does not want to be made known to, and there is no one place where a believer should not go and aim to make disciples. This is not something men can do on their own accord, which is why Jesus says: "I am with you always." The Great Commission, the command for believers, is not left without a promise. What God has purposed, will be accomplished; He will be *exalted among the nations* (Psalm 46) because He is unfailing and His mission is unfailing, and because He promises to be with us as we live out His mission, why would we hold back in joining Him?

In conclusion of this chapter; Jesus says to teach all the disciples to obey everything He commanded, and one of the things He commanded, and one of the things that we teach people, is disciples are to go to all the world and teach. Each believer should be involved; even if indirectly. As we consider what "The Great Commission" is and why it matters, we must ask ourselves: *Does it matter if someone hears the Gospel in their lifetime?* If the Gospel is how eternal salvation is received, and we are given the call to share this salvation, the Great Commission should matter to us. We must continue to act as ambassadors for Christ, and "we plead on Christ's behalf: "Be reconciled to God" (2 Corinthians 5:20). God's ultimate plan is revealed in Revelation 7:9, which states,

> *"After this, I looked and there before me was a great multitude that no one could count, from every nation, tribe, people and language, standing before the throne and in front of the Lamb. They were wearing white robes and were holding palm branches in their hands."*

One day, we will stand before God, praising His holy name with all of the nations (all the people). What a joy and freedom it will be to know that each of us played a small role in hearing His name exalted in new languages, tribes, and people. If a church is not reaching non-believers, baptizing them, teaching them to obey Jesus' commands, and taking the gospel to the nations; they are not doing the Great Commission. Similar to many; they may actually be only talking about "The Great Commission. If our family, friends, and others do not learn to live out the Great Commission and share their faith, there may be people in their lives who will face eternal condemnation, as a consequence.

NOTES:

Chapter 6

SAY THE RIGHT THING AT THE RIGHT TIME

What we say really matters; Ephesians 4:29, is a verse that would bring an extensive or all-encompassing change in all of our relationships; if, we would apply it carefully or conscientiously.

> Ephesians 4:29 (ESV), says: *"Stop all your dirty talk. "Say the right thing at the right time" and help others by what you say."*

> Ephesians 4:29 (NASB), says, *"Let no unwholesome word proceed from your mouth, but only such a word as is good for edification according to the need of the moment, so that it will give grace to those who hear."*

This scripture basically tells Christians to avoid speaking words that are unwholesome, corrupt, or harmful to others. Instead, Christians should speak words that are good, edifying, and gracious to those who hear. Ephesians 4:29, shows the importance of controlling the tongue and using it for God's glory and the benefit of others. Instead of using "corrupting" or negative talk; the apostle Paul provides two rules or guidelines for how to speak.

One, we are to speak in beneficial (helpful) ways about meaningful things, and Two, we are to speak in ways appropriate to the situation we are in.

Speak in ways appropriate to the situation we are in; what might be completely acceptable in one situation, might be rude or unkind in another. The goal is to show grace (mercy) to those who are listening to our words. We are not supposed to prioritize our own feelings, but make it our intent to help others through our words. We are not to let any foul (filthy) words come out of your mouth. Only say what is helpful when it is needed for building up the community so that it benefits those who hear what you say.

As for an example; name calling. Probably one of the most concerning effects of name-calling, is what it can do to a person's mental health. Name-calling is abusive, derogatory language, or insults. It is a form of relational or personal, bullying. Sadly, this behavior is common among kids. Name-calling, which is sometimes dismissed as teasing or ribbing, is often present in sibling (brother or sister) bullying. However, this type of talk is very hurtful and can harm a child's sense of self (personality or character). Name-calling makes it difficult for victims to trust their perceptions or views about themselves.

Name-calling hurts in the moment, and can have many lasting repercussions or impacts. Many hate crimes; begin with name-calling and escalate to violence.

Parents, please never ignore name-calling! Name-calling destroys the parent-child bond. It can distance a child from both parents; crush a youngster's self-esteem, break-down communication, change a child's brain structure, and it can be remembered and continue to hurt or damage a person, into his or her future.

Words perpetrate or cause Harm; especially unpleasant or unwholesome words. There were a lot of hurtful words being thrown around the church in Ephesus. It was apparently occurring between the Messianic Jews and the Gentiles. When we use our words to inflict or cause harm in the church; it causes lasting damage. The apostle Paul reminds all of us that we are to lead with grace, and love when we speak to others. We don't know what the other person may be going through, and we can only make the situation better by speaking helpful or wholesome words.

Giving grace is becoming, a lost art form. To extend grace means, we overlook what someone says, and see behind it. Another way to look at it is to give others the benefit of the doubt.

Giving someone "the benefit of the doubt," means you assume someone's actions are honest and well-intentioned until proven otherwise, rather than jumping to a negative conclusion right away. When someone doesn't measure up to your expectations how you think they should get it wrong or slip up on the side of grace.

When we speak unwholesome words, it throws, gas on the fire! You may be the only one who shines the light of Jesus into their life. Words do hurt, more than sticks and stones; words can build up or tear down! Edification is the process of us using our words to build others up. The dictionary definition for edification is: "improvement, instruction, or enlightenment, especially when morally or spiritually uplifting." Edification then, is similar to spiritual growth; it moves us forward in knowledge of and obedience to God. Look for ways to encourage people, be sincere because everyone can detect smooth talk or flattery, encourage others on to good works by being the example.

It's important to say the right thing or words at the right time. A well-timed word can push or propel someone through the storm they are navigating. Parents and teachers play a huge role in the life of a child. Young children mimic what their parents say or do at birth. The parents form the foundation of what the child becomes early on.

The teachings of the parents influence the personality and choices of the child thereafter. When the child goes to school; they meet the teachers who also have a major role to impart knowledge in them. The parents and the teachers can teach and influence the children to hate corruption. They can instil or inspire the values of hard work and determination and the benefits of reaping what they sow. With such values, the children will grow appreciating the need for integrity (honesty). Transparency, accountability, and hard work will form the basis of their lives. If we have a majority of them working in government as adults, then they may instil or inspire the same values and reform the corrupt government system.

We must let our words "give grace" to those who hear. Words can hurt and harm, and words can heal, and help! Realize how hurtful, your words can be. It is very easy to post a comment(s) on Facebook, Twitter, or Instagram without putting much thought into it. It only takes a few seconds to send a text message. It is easy to make a sarcastic remark or make fun of someone. It is very easy to hurt someone with words. It is not necessarily physical blows that are the most harmful; words can reduce a person's self-esteem to next to nothing, in an instant. Text messages that tell you that no one cares about you, or that no one likes you because of how you look, are hard to face. The damage can last for years. Maybe actually meant as a joke; maybe the person sending text messages was together with some friends when he or she wrote it, and was pressured into it. Maybe several other people share, the same opinion, and someone feels like he or she deserves to know the truth. These are flat excuses!

Regardless of the intention; we should never say or send a message that can be interpreted in this way. This is one of the great dangers with social media. Words do not disappear; They continue to exist from the moment you say them or send that message. They exist in the thoughts and mind of the recipient, and also in God's memory. This applies to good and evil, because God is a righteous judge. (Matthew 12:37)

In conclusion, let us not say or write anything we would not repeat, but stop and think again before we laugh at someone or make sarcastic comments. But if we do say words we regret, the best thing we can do, is make it right. Ask for forgiveness; asking for forgiveness can be hard, and requires courage. We all need forgiveness, most of all from God Himself (Ephesians 4:32).

When we pray for this from a true and honest heart, then God is good and forgives us of all kinds of sin, even thoughtless words. But we also need to make it right with those we have hurt. Then we can pray that God gives us a new mind, and pray to start over so that the same thing doesn't happen again. The intention is we become so transformed that those kinds of words no longer come out of us.

We will give an account to God for every sinful word we speak (Matthew 12:36). God will use our words to justify or condemn us (Matthew 12:37) Our words reveal the condition of our hearts (Matthew 12:34-35). Corrupt talk is the opposite of gospel talk (Ephesians 4:29). Foolish words are the opposite of thanksgiving (Ephesians 5:4). Our words have the power to destroy another person (Proverbs 18:21).

"Death and life are in the power of the tongue." In Scripture, words range from "Father, forgive them" to *"What is truth?"* and from *"Did God really say?"* to *"It is finished!"* Words affect both time and eternity. Our words have the power to build up another person (Proverbs 18:21). The more we talk, the more we are prone to sin (Proverbs 10:19). It is wise to talk less and listen more (James 1:19-20). Our words should give grace to those who hear.

NOTES:

Chapter 7

YOU MUST KNOW THE WORD FOR YOURSELF

Everything God gives us has responsibility attached that expect those gifts to be used wisely and carefully to bring glory to God, and light to the lost. We as children of Go d, now have direct access to Him. We don't have to pray through anybody else, confess through anybody else, and we don't have to fellowship with God through anybody else. God's word says, if we say we have fellowship with him, and walk in the darkness, we lie, and do not the truth" (1 John 1:6). We must read the Bible for ourself; talk with the Lord and fellowship directly with Him. We cannot take everyone else's word for the word of God; we have to know it for ourself.

> Deuteronomy 29:29 (ESV), says *"The secret things belong to the Lord our God, but the things that are revealed belong to us and to our children forever, that we may do all the words of this law."*

God does have a plan for you; He created you with a specific purpose in mind and equipped you with the gifts you need to fulfill that purpose, but He has not hidden His will from you; at least not in the sense that you have to go "find it." We won't be held accountable for what we do not know or for things which we couldn't have known. There are just some aspects of God's will that is only for God to know but what has been revealed, those things we are accountable for, namely (specifically) the Word (Bible) of God. You have also been gifted for ministry to serve other people. You are made to fellowship with God. And not only do we fellowship with God, and share in communion with Him, but we are unified to one another in fellowship.

If you want to do God's will, obey His Word and if God reveals more of His will for your life, such as a calling or a specific purpose; obey that as well. But you don't have to stress over things which He has not revealed. If God has a specific calling for your life; He will reveal it in His own time. But even if you don't feel God revealing His will for your life, He has a way of directing our steps as we obey his word. God does this through our obedience, through inspiration, through gifts He has given us, and people He puts in our path. Sorry to say that so many Christians are concerned about God's will, calling or purpose for their lives, but they won't even read or study the Bible to find out what it says about His will. Also, there are other Christians who know what the Word of God says, but refuse to live in obedience to His will. But they are so concerned about God's calling for their lives.

We will all be judged according to the knowledge of the truth we have access to. We are in a time, where knowing the Word of God for ourself is beyond important.

> A great example is Joshua 1:8 (KJV), *"This book of the law shall not depart out of thy mouth; but thou shalt meditate therein day and night, that thou mayest observe to do according to all that is written therein: for then thou shalt make thy way prosperous, and then thou shalt have good success."*

All Scripture is the Word of God and Joshua was an example of a godly man who both believed God's Word and acted upon it. Joshua knew the value of hearing God's Word and meditating upon it. He knew that neglecting the Word of the Lord was a recipe for disaster and like Mary of Bethany. Joshua learned the one thing that was needful, to listen to the voice of the Lord and to meditate upon all that He has said day and night. And like them, we too need to consider it in our hearts and talk about it to other believers. Just like Joshua, we would be wise to take heed to God's Word, to recite His Word using our mind, to keep the truth of His Word forever on our lips and in our hearts, and to observe all that God has written to us in our lives. Then we will prosper and succeed in whatsoever we do, to our benefit and to His glory!

Sometimes we misunderstand what it means, 'to succeed' or 'to prosper' which has given rise to a prosperity teaching which places the emphasis on temporal, worldly prosperity rather than eternal spiritual wealth. God may choose to bestow or give worldly wealth on His children or He may permit the alternative, but the goods and chattel of this world are passing away, and like the apostle Paul, we need to be content in all things. What is important, is to know the Word of God, to trust the Word of God, and to apply the Word of God in every circumstance of life. We should read, mark, learn, and inwardly digest the Word of the Lord. We should study God's Book of instruction; particularly those passages that relate specifically to the Church, and we should continually feed on God's Word in our hearts by faith with thanksgiving. We should meditate on God's Word, memorize His Word, trust His Word, love His Word, and we should be sure to obey His Word and apply His Word in our daily lives. Doing so, we will certainly prosper and succeed in all we do, to His praise and glory.

In conclusion, a certain way of never knowing God's will for your life is to not live obedience to His word. It's essential to walk in obedience to God's Word and trust that He will take care of the rest. If you don't already know God's will for your life; find out what God has to say so that you can walk in obedience to His will. Pray and read your Bible.

NOTES:

Chapter 8

TIME FOR GOD'S PEOPLE TO RECOMMIT

Hebrews 10:25 (NKJV), says *"²⁵not forsaking the assembling of ourselves together, as is the manner of some, but exhorting one another, and so much the more as you see the Day approaching."*

"¹⁸And I also say to you that "you are Peter, and on this rock I will build My church, and ᵖthe gates of Hades shall not ⁷prevail against it" (Matthew 16:18; NKJV).

Anyone who accepts Jesus Christ as Savior and Lord becomes a part of "the people of God. The relationship does not come through church attendance or good deeds. It is a deliberate choice to follow God alone. That's why 2 Corinthians 6:16 and Mark 8:38 both indicate or point out that a choice has to be made. And when we make that choice to embrace God, He embraces us as well; then we truly are His people. In virtually, every sermon or message I preach or teach; I may say or call the people under the sound of my voice, "saints of God. In the Word of God (the Bible); "the people of God" are often called "saints!"

Fellow believers who live a holy and godly life in Christ Jesus are the ones I am referring too. When I call them saints or "saints of God" (the people of God), we are either Saints or "Ain'ts"? In other words, if you are "saved," or "born again," you are a saint; if not, you "Ain't!"

In Matthew 16:18, Jesus responds to Peter's confession that He is the Christ, the Son of the Living God. Jesus declares that He will build His Church on this truth, and that the gates of hell will not prevail against it. This means that the Church will be victorious over Satan and his forces. The forces of evil will not be able to conquer the people of God, and the gospel will be preserved and proclaimed.

It's time for many of God's People to recommit. God's people are those who always have a clear or pure relationship with Him. The main purpose of this chapter is to let God's people know, it's time for us as genuine believers and church to return to a biblical (holy) commitment to the house of God. The house of God, the dwelling place of God; is the church which is built by Christ growing in the believers and making His home in their hearts (Ephesians 2:21-22).

God told David that only Christ can build His house and that He does not want a physical house of cedar. God wants a house built by Christ coming and building Himself into us. God does not want us to do anything; He wants Christ to make His home in our heart so that we with all the believers, could be His eternal dwelling place; the church. Together, we are the Body of Christ, and we must be connected together, and be connected to the head, Jesus, to be effective in our mission on earth. God's Word teaches the importance of active participation in a church. Believers must make church attendance a priority in their personal and family schedules, and put going to church ahead of other seemingly or beneficial activities. There was a time when church attendance was an important or principal focal point of our homes, a community's culture and calendar. Families would make it a priority to attend church services and functions or activities virtually every time the church's "doors were open."

Times have definitely changed; just look around you. The majority of Americans no longer attend church on a weekly basis and many of today's "practicing" Christians only attend one church service per month. Things or influences for the decline in church attendance are diverse or worldwide but include the availability of religious content on-line, the flood or increase of other activities for family members on weekends (like the propensity and popularity of youth sports), and the general increase of a more secular (nonspiritual or worldly) mindset for many Americans. The church is God's idea and the church is His plan for this era or age. The most important reason for the "people of God" to attend church is the church is God's idea: Jesus said, *"I will build My church, and the gates of Hades (hell) shall not prevail against it"* (Matthew 16:18)

It's time for "God's people" to recommit themselves to active and regular participation in church. It's time for genuine believers in Christ Jesus, to make church a priority in their personal and family schedules again. In Matthew 16:18, Jesus said, *"I will build My church, and the gates of Hades shall not prevail against it."* This is God's idea for us to attend church, not mines, yours, or anyone else. We are living in the in the doctrine of the New Testament time; the church is how God is accomplishing His work on earth today. The church is God's plan and must be a top priority in our lives. Hebrews 10:25 (NKJV) states, *"[25] not forsaking the assembling of ourselves together, as is the manner (way, behavior, conduct) of some, but exhorting one another, and so much the more as you see the Day approaching."*

God wants His people to be actively involved in the church. The church is where God's people are taught God's Word so they can grow spiritually. Yes, it's true that followers of Christ can and should study the Word on their own, but learning under the sound preaching and teaching ministry of pastors and other church leaders is essential for one's spiritual growth. It's time for us as a church to return to a biblical commitment to the house of God. Together, we are the Body of Christ and we must be connected together, and be connected to the head, Jesus Christ to be effective in our mission on earth. It's important that we attend church on a regular basis and practice our God given spiritual gifts. Trust me; every believer has at least one or more spiritual gifts that's godly-given to effectively serve God in the church.

So many people now desire to be lone-rangers or spectators. God never intended the church to be for spectators or those who just show up for entertainment or a performance on a Sunday morning. God designed His church to be a place for believers to participate in church functions by utilizing their spiritual gifts, either in a public setting or privately with other believers. It's important for us as believers to grow spiritually; ignorance of the law is not an excuse! People perish due to a lack of knowledge (Hosea 4:6); therefore, ignorance is not bliss (not pleasure or happiness). Spiritual ignorance, is very dangerous! It's time for God's people to recommit; there is power in consistency and Commitment. Spiritual growth is not automatic; it's not something you just desire. You have to be committed and show-up consistently.

We needed revival; it is important that revivals take place because they help us have an awakening and renewal to the Lord. Revivals helps us to desire to know God better and to grow in our relationship with Him. Revivals also convict us of our own sin and can be a means or a catalyst to repentance in our own lives. We never need to underestimate what a revival is capable of doing. The Holy Spirit is at work in revivals, and He can help awaken our souls and renew our minds to have the same desire and love we had for Jesus when we first became believers. The purpose of a church revival is to allow the power of the Holy Spirit to transform both believers and nonbelievers alike. Through revival meetings; people sense the power of God and are called to prayer and repentance.

In conclusion, so many people have drifted away or drifting away from the Lord, Jesus Christ. If you fall in either category; drifted away or drifting away, you probably haven't spent a lot of time talking to Jesus through prayer lately. It's time to reconnect with God through prayer. Prayer is one of the best ways to reconnect with God. In prayer; you get the chance to have a two-way conversation with God. Your Prayer does not have to be elaborate, complicated or fancy. Start your conversation with God by confessing your sins to Jesus and asking for forgiveness. Be honest with God; tell him what you are becoming aware of. Use your own words, like this: Lord Jesus, thank you for loving me. Talk to God; you can do this freely and with ease in your own words.

NOTES:

Chapter 9

REMEMBER WHERE OUR TRUE HOME IS

Philippians 3:20, says, *"But our citizenship is in heaven. And we eagerly await a Savior from there, the Lord Jesus Christ."*

Philippians 3:20, is a scripture or verse from the New Testament that expresses the Christian belief that their true home and allegiance, is in heaven. Christian belief that their true home and allegiance, is in heaven, where they expect the Lord Jesus Christ to come from, as their Savior. Philippians 3:20, is translated differently in several versions of the Bible, but the main idea is the same. This chapter to enlighten you and others on the importance of understanding that this world we live in; is not our home. Our real home is in heaven, and our citizenship is in heaven.

Because of our profession of faith in Christ Jesus; our behavior or conduct should be different than those who do not know God, and our primary focus should be on eternal things rather than worldly or temporal passions. Our earthly home, offers temporary and imperfect comfort. While we can enjoy times of rest and relaxation at home; there are responsibilities as well. There is always work to be done! Our heavenly home offers eternal and perfect comfort. Revelation 21:4, says, heaven is described as a place in which God *"will wipe away every tear from their eyes; and there will no longer be any death; there will no longer be any mourning, or crying, or pain; the first things have passed away"*

God will *"wipe away every tear,"* meaning the pain from this life; will be perfectly comforted. There will also be no cause of pain in the future for eternity – as all things that had caused sorrow, will have *"passed away."* Our home in heaven is far greater or superior than any home we might have here, on the earth. so, we all need to *"remember, where our true home is."* In Philippians 3:20, the apostle Paul wrote, *"For our citizenship is in heaven, from which also we eagerly wait for a Savior, the Lord Jesus Christ."* We must recognize that we are strangers and pilgrims on the earth. This recognition should cause us to live in a certain way.

> The apostle Peter wrote in 1 Peter 2: 11-12: *"Beloved, I urge you as aliens and strangers to abstain from fleshly lusts which wage war against the soul. Keep your behavior excellent among the Gentiles."*

Understanding that our home is in heaven, God expects us to keep from sin and engage in good works. We also need to remember that we will be judged for how we have lived as pilgrims on the earth.

The apostle Paul said in 2 Corinthians 5:9-10:

> *"Therefore, we also have as our ambition, whether at home or absent, to be pleasing to Him. For we must all appear before the judgment seat of Christ, so that each one may be recompensed (rewarded) for his deeds in the body, according to what he has done, whether good or bad."*

So, our conduct, is not something to be taken lightly; also, as we live here on the earth; we must use our time, wisely. Paul said, *"Therefore be careful how you walk, not as unwise men but as wise, making the most of your time, because the days are evil"* (Ephesians 5:15-16).

To make the most of our time, we must fill it with *"fruitful labor"* (Philippians 1:22), wherever we are so that we can please the Lord! I pray that this chapter will help many to understand, we must never lose sight of the fact that "our citizenship is in heaven" (Philippians 3:20). But also understand that we must live in such a way that we will get there. Living for God may be difficult, but it is not joyless! But we must live in such a way that we will get to our home and our citizenship, in heaven.

Jesus said we do this by doing the will of God (Matthew 7:21). When we get to the end of our earthly journey, we do not want to hear: *"I never knew you, depart from Me, you who practice lawlessness"* (Matthew 7:23). We must stay busy serving the Lord so that we can reach the home in heaven that God has promised to the faithful.

Philippians 3:20, says, *"But "our citizenship is in heaven." And we eagerly await a Savior from there, the Lord Jesus Christ."* I want to focus or express a bit more on "Citizenship." Citizenship is the state of being a citizen of a particular country or region. It entails or involves certain rights, responsibilities, and privileges. Citizens are expected to obey the laws of their country and to participate in its government. Citizens are also entitled to certain benefits, such as: protection from the government, access to social services, and the right to vote. When we talk about citizenship; it's usually in the context or perspective of earthly matters, such as: possessions, rights, and obligations. But I want to make sure, if one doesn't know the need to understand, the Biblical teachings on citizenship, (heavenly and earthly citizenship).

The Bible teaches that we are all citizens of heaven. Christians need to remember though we are in this world; we are not, of this world. **Thank God!** Our ultimate citizenship, is in heaven, eagerly wait. In Philippians 3:20, the apostle Paul presents a direct contrast or comparison to the earthly focus of the enemies, of the Cross in verse 19.

> *Philippians 3:19 (NIV), states, "Their destiny is destruction, their god is their stomach, and their glory is in their shame. Their mind is set on earthly things."*

In verse 19, destruction; indicates the opposite of eternal salvation. The things in which they take pride actually are the things that will bring "disgrace" or "humiliation" to them. Things of which they should have been ashamed. The eager desire of Christians is not earthly things, but a heavenly person; the savior, the Lord, Jesus Christ.

The context of Philippians 3:19-20, is important because prior to Paul's revelation of this truth, he speaks of those who "walk as enemies of the cross." These individuals were more concerned about temporal matters and personal pleasure than Jesus Christ. The apostle Paul said of them, *"Their destiny is destruction, their god is their stomach, and their glory is in their shame. Their mind is set on earthly things"* (Philippians 3:19).

Set your mind on the things above, not on the things that are on earth. The Amplified Bible, says: Set your mind and keep focused habitually on the things above (the heavenly things), not on earthly THINGS! In order to be a citizen of heaven; you must have faith in Jesus Christ, and accept Him as your Savior. To be a citizen of heaven, is to see your connection with Jesus as the most important part of your life. You must serve the Lord above all else! Any earthly citizenship you or we may enjoy, is understood only through the lens of our primary heavenly citizenship.

Many of us know and understand that a passport is a very important document required to travel out of the United States of America to international or foreign countries. Well, our Lord, and Savior, Jesus Christ came from that life to the earth to make it possible for us to go to heaven. Jesus came to overcome evil, and did so by dying on the Cross and rising again. **Jesus** said that, *"if you believe in me, you will share my life forever"* (John 6:40; 11:26); that belief, that faith in Jesus is the only guaranteed passport to heaven. Our heavenly citizenship is not defined by the color of our passport; it is well-defined by who we as believers in Christ Jesus. When you accepted Jesus Christ into your life; you were automatically issued an indefinite passport from heaven. Those who are serving God wholeheartedly, know that our heavenly home is made up of an eternal and perfect family.

In Matthew 10: 34-36; Jesus warned about the possibility or likelihood that serving Him would put us in opposition to our earthly families: Jesus said, *"Do not think that I came to bring peace on earth; I did not come to bring peace, but a sword. For I came to set a man against his father, and a daughter against her mother, and a daughter-in-law against her mother-in-law; and a man's enemies will be the members of his household."*

I am sure we all can relate to this scripture Matthew 10: 34-36. Even if none of our earthly family is in heaven with us, our spiritual family will be there. We have the great privilege through the love of the Father to be "children of God" (1 John 3:1). Jesus said, *"For whoever does the will of My Father who is in heaven, he is My brother and sister and mother"* (Matthew 12:50). We are all brothers and sisters and have the blessing of being God's children. We will all be together in heaven.

God does not want us to face death uncertain, about our future. If we place our faith in Jesus Christ; we can know with absolute certainty that we are going to be welcomed into Heaven.

In conclusion, I always emphasize to my church congregation, family, friends, associates, and many others to please not play around or mess around with their spiritual or heavenly citizenship. Our lives genuine believers should be conformed to the glory of our citizenship. They are holy in heaven, and we must be too. Pretending or faking will void or cancel one's citizenship in heaven. A person's spiritual passport will be invalid and denied.

The Bible tells us that our entry into heavenly citizenship is like being born again (John 3:3; Matthew 3:2; 7:21; Romans 14:17). I personally like to keep real because God, always keep it real. God definitely knows the difference between those who belong to Him and those who only appear to belong to Him. There are those who act like citizens of heaven, but have no personal relationship with Jesus and have not experienced a rebirth in their hearts (Matthew 7:21). Please always encourage yourself and others to not play games with God! Be encouraged to read 1 Corinthians 7:6-11; don't let the culture or society dictate your actions and determine, how you live your life. If you are a true follower of Christ; you should live differently, not try to find ways around God's design. Don't play games with God; He loves you too much, to let you win! Life is not a game, and there are consequences how we run the race.

NOTES:

Chapter 10

THE OLD HAS GONE THE NEW IS HERE

> *"¹⁷Therefore, if anyone is in Christ, the new creation has come: The old has gone, the new is here"* (2 Corinthians 5:17)

Second Corinthians 5:17, is one of the most well-known passages in Paul's letters to Corinth, and perhaps in the entire Bible: *"Therefore, if anyone is in Christ, the new creation has come: The old has gone, the new is HERE!"*

God wants us to grow by affirming our acceptance through Christ Jesus. We are a new being, a new creation made possible through the suffering of Christ Jesus on our behalf. You enter into new experiences of God's love as you accept by faith that which God has done in Christ Jesus. The new creation is described in 2 Corinthians 5:17: *"Therefore, if anyone is in Christ, he is a new creation; the old has gone, the new has come!"*

The word "therefore" refers us back to verses 14-16 in 2 Corinthians, Chapter 5, where the apostle Paul tells us that all believers in Christ Jesus have died with Him and no longer live for themselves.

> *"¹⁴For Christ's love compels us, because we are convinced that one died for all, and therefore all died. ¹⁵And he died for all, that those*

who live should no longer live for themselves but for him who died for them and was raised again. ¹⁶So from now on we regard no one from a worldly point of view. Though we once regarded Christ in this way, we do so no longer."

The new man in Christ Jesus is the creature that is birthed from the union of God and man in Christ. You become a new man, not because God does something to you, but you become a new man because Christ is in you! All that you are, is a direct result of being one with Jesus Christ. Being in Christ is one way of describing what it means to be a Christian. Those who are "in Christ" are spiritually united or connected to and identified with Christ such that all the blessings and the benefits obtained by Christ, belong to them.

Our greatest need as believers is to stay deeply connected with Christ (John 15:4-10). He desires us to know, commune and fellowship with Him on a moment-by-moment basis. The more you know who you are in Christ Jesus, the more your behavior will reflect your true identity.

"Do not be conformed to this world, but be transformed by the renewing of your mind" (Romans 12:2).

To live an effective Christian life, you need to KNOW and BELIEVE who you are in Christ Jesus. The Christian life is all about changing; we should always be willing to move to the right, but never to the left. In other words, we should be willing to make improvements, but never compromise our convictions and character. Change will always happen! There seems to always, be a guarantee in life that change will occur or happen, whether we want it to or not. Change is something we tend to fear, and become anxious about because we do not feel in control of life. The good news is; God has a plan for your life and mines that includes hope, future, and prosperity. We need to learn to trust in God and "allow the change to grow us" to become more like Jesus Christ.

We are promised that all things will work together for good for those who love Him and keep His commandments. God is walking this life journey with you; His presence is always with you, guiding you. The apostle Paul has written that Christ's death for sin has changed the way He regards people. Instead of looking at each person as a plain human being, he must view those who are in Christ Jesus as something totally different. Those who are "in Christ" are those who have faith in Him, credited with Christ's righteous life, and their sin forgiven by Christ's death in their place. Such people are new creatures; those "in Christ" have become something they were not before. Their identity has changed from being the fallen version of themselves, to being associated with the righteousness of Christ. That's who they are now!

In fact, the old version of a Christian, who they were before they were "in Christ," is not recoverable. The old is gone, Paul writes. The new has come! All the old dreams and ideas and agendas and purposes have ceased to exist, and have been replaced by Christ's ideas and agendas and purposes in an entirely new creature called "Christian." The apostle Paul's words are true in another way; the old way of humanity is also gone. The old way of the law (mosaic LAW) is also gone. Christ is the long-promised new Covenant that makes it possible for men and women to be made new once and for all, and for eternity, with no possibility of returning to the old.

I stated earlier as believers; we should be living for Jesus Christ? We all live for something. As parents we live for our children. Spouses may live for each other, and business owners, may live for return on investments (ROI) or success. We say that we are "living for" something when that is the motivation for all we do. Living for Jesus means that pleasing Him is our highest aim or goal (Colossians 1:10). Although we have dozens of lesser motivators, those filled with the Spirit of Christ Jesus are motivated primarily by His goals and His plans for their lives. When those plans collide or crash with smaller goals; those who are living for Jesus follow His way and not their own (Proverbs 3:5–6).

The expression or phrase "living for Jesus," can sound rather strange or unrealistic. But Jesus warned that living for Him would be costly (Luke 14:26–33). The first disciples were willing to pay that price. They suffered tremendous persecution and even death, in order to glorify God (Acts 5:41). Stephen was stoned (Acts 7:58–60), James was beheaded (Acts 12:2), and history records that all the apostles but John were also martyred.

> Martyred means: *a person who voluntarily suffers death as the penalty of witnessing to and refusing to renounce (quit or forsake) a religion.*

A person who sacrifices something of great value and especially life itself for the sake of principle a martyr to the cause of freedom. Even these days, as I speak; Christians around the world are beaten, robbed, tortured, and imprisoned, simply because they live for Jesus.

In conclusion, people who live for Jesus are not as concerned about earthly treasures or material possessions the way the rest of the world. Although we are free to enjoy all God's blessings in this life; Jesus made it very clear that we are not to put our whole focus on them (Matthew 6:19–20). People who are living for Jesus, focus on eternity and dedicate themselves to endeavors that have eternal significance. Worldly entanglements are temporary, and seem like wasted time and effort. Our passion and energy are directed toward investing in the lives of others who will join us in heaven one day (Luke 10:2–3). Jesus made His requirements very clear: *"If anyone would come after me, let him deny himself, take up his cross daily and follow me"* (Luke 9:23).

NOTES:

Chapter 11

WHICH LIFE DO YOU WANT?

There are many people who think they can just go to or have heaven without having Jesus. They want the glory, but they don't want to be concerned or bothered by the cross, much less the One who died on the cross, name JESUS! There are people who will be rejected or prohibited from entering the kingdom of God! Some people may be found on their local church membership rolls, but they will not be found in Heaven's rolls. Their names will be absent from the Book of Life.

Romans 6:23, states, *"For the wages of sin is death, but the gift of God is eternal life in Christ Jesus, our Lord."* This scripture many times are used to alarm or frighten people about hell and encourage them about heaven. But do people really want to go to Heaven? People have a lot of ideas about how to get to heaven; many of them may perhaps think that all one has to do is be a good person, go to church, or help others in order to Go or make it To Heaven.

So many people are being misled by false teachers and false teaching. The Bible is true and exceptionally clear; there is only one way to heaven, and that's through Jesus Christ. Furthermore, the Bible teaches that the only way to get to heaven is to believe that Jesus, is the Son of God. It's important to accept that one cannot go to heaven unless they become saved in Christ. Yes, we all have sinned or done something wrong, and those sins separate us from God. In the Old Testament of the Bible, people were commanded to make animal sacrifices so they would be forgiven for their sins. However, the New Testament says that God sent His son Jesus to Earth to be killed as the ultimate sacrifice, so that all, not some, but all people could be forgiven, if they accepted Jesus Christ. Plus, the Bible says, Jesus was raised from the dead 3 days after He was killed, proving His divine nature.

> John 3:16 describes God's gift to humankind: *"For God so loved the world, that He gave his only Son, that whoever believes in him should not perish but have eternal life."*

Romans 5:8, describes the sacrifice Jesus made for sinners:

> *"But God shows his love for us in that while we were still sinners, Christ died for us."*

It is important that all people understand they cannot go to heaven, unless they become saved in Christ. The Bible says in John 14:6: *"Jesus said to him: "I am the way, and the truth, and the life. No one comes to the Father except through me."*

This means, prior to becoming a follower or disciple of Jesus Christ, one has to let go of the idea that there are other paths or ways to heaven. IT's NOT! The only way you can fully understand the significance of Jesus' sacrifice and the importance of worshipping Him is to go through Him to get to heaven. The Bible makes it very clear that we cannot be good enough to get into heaven on our own; it's not something that can be accomplished or achieved by our "works," or actions.

> Ephesians 2:8-9, says, *"For it is by grace you have been saved, through faith—and this not from yourselves, it is the gift of God— not by works, so that no one can boast."*

Merely acknowledging that Jesus is the Son of God and He died for our sins, is not enough to get anyone into heaven. You have to make a conscious decision or choice to become a follower of Jesus; praying to God for forgiveness, for your sins. This is well-known in Christianity as being "born again," because your life should be different from that moment forward.

In John 3:3, the Bible clearly confirms that you cannot go to heaven without doing this: *Jesus answered to him, "Truly, truly, I say to you, unless one is born again, he cannot see the kingdom of God."*

The late reverend, Billy Graham said: "Those who believe they will end up in Heaven without belonging to Christ should make their peace with God today. There are actually some people who declare or proclaim they have no desire to go to Heaven because they believe it will be boring. Some truly think that hell will be a big party. They imagine that Heaven will be a place where harps are played upon the lofty clouds. Most people want to believe they will go to Heaven upon death because they don't want to consider or think about, the alternative. But they must face the truth and receive Christ. Heaven will be filled only with those who belong to Jesus Christ, for those who: follow Him, obey Him, and love Him, and Heaven is the place that Jesus is preparing for them."

Jesus said, *"I go and prepare a place for you, that where I am, there you may be also"* (John 14:3). This is a wonderful promise from Jesus Christ, Himself. But what does Romans 6:23, really mean by saying: *"For the wages of sin is death, but the gift of God is eternal life in Christ Jesus, our Lord."*

The apostle Paul sums up this section of his letter, and the entire gospel, in this one famous verse. He compares or contrast the two types of lives he has been describing. First, those without Christ are slaves to sin, Secondly, become servants of righteousness, by trusting in Christ. Those without Christ are slaves to sin; their work of sinfulness earns wages of death. In other words; they earn eternal death, eternal separation from God. No matter how good a person may think they are; their work can never be good enough (Isaiah 64:6), and in the end; they have only themselves to blame for sinning against God (Romans 1:18–20; 3:10, 23).

Become servants of righteousness by trusting in Christ. The apostle Paul has described the possibility that we can become servants of righteousness by trusting in Christ. This is not something we can do on our own. The apostle Paul wrote in Romans 3:23, that all have sinned and fall short of God's glory. No, eternal life can only be given; it cannot be earned by human beings (Ephesians 2:8–9). The apostle Paul describes eternal life as God's free gift in Christ Jesus, our Lord. When we trust in Christ, God gives us credit for Christ's perfect, sinless life and accepts the payment of Christ's death for our sin. The result, eternal life with Christ Jesus, sharing in His glory, is given to us as a gift. The apostle Paul appears to be asking, "Which life do you want?" Which is also, the title of this chapter: "WHICH LIFE DO YOU WANT?" It's your choice; you get to choose which life you want to live. Life is a gift from God! Every day when He allows you to wake up, you have something important or meaningful to do. Sometimes it may not seem like you don't have something important or meaningful to do. Sometimes you may wander without purpose, feeling lost, believing that your life has no purpose. You may feel like you are stuck in a "hole or confusion" where you know you should do more with the life God has given you, but you don't know where to start! You often wonder what God wants you to do, with the life He's given you. If that's you, know that God wants you to live a life filled with purpose. God wants you to live a life filled with worship for Him. Glory to God! God wants you to win souls for Him to save; use your God-given gift! God wants you to live a life filled with peace and joy. I am speaking of peace and joy that only God can bring, to fill your life.

In conclusion, the apostle Paul explains that sin results in death, but God gives the gift of eternal life. The phrase eternal life is used 42 times in the New Testament, and usually refers to something we receive as a gift at the moment of belief of the gospel. But 11 of these 42 times, eternal life is presented as something to be attained. In order to attain or obtain eternal life, we must have an active and growing relationship with Jesus Christ, Himself. We do this through living in faith and obedience, Christians can fully enjoy God's free gift of eternal life. We avoid the "wages of sin" and escape the spiritual death.

We must place our faith in Christ. Only He can save us (John 14:16). Then, out of our trust in Him and our love for Him (in response to His love for us; 1 John 4:19). Our obedience leads us to a more vibrant experience of true life (John 10:10). The apostle Paul wrote in Romans 6:22, *"But now that you have been set free from sin and have become slaves of God, the fruit you get leads to sanctification and its end, eternal life."*

As Christ-followers; we are free to live in obedience to God and undergo the process of sanctification. As part of that sanctification, we begin to experience eternal life even while on this earth (John 10:10; John 15:11). And, ultimately, we will spend eternity with God in heaven. Glory to God!

NOTES:

Chapter 12

SHOW GOD, YOU LOVE HIM!

In this brief but powerful final chapter of my book; I desire to encourage you and many others worldwide to truly show God love. Showing love to God is a good thing because without God, we would not have anything; especially, food, clothing, shelter, family, children, wife, husband, etc. It's really very hard for many to understand the love God has for us while we were and are still sinners. It's true, God absolutely love us unconditionally!

Deuteronomy 6: 5 (NKJV), says, *"⁵You shall love the LORD your God with all your heart, with all your soul, and with all your strength."*

This is the greatest commandment!

It's important that we show God, we love Him. I Love the Lord! To love the Lord means to choose Him for an intimate or personal relationship, and to obey His commands. This command, to love Him is given often throughout Deuteronomy (chapter 6, but other chapters in Deuteronomy, like: 7:9, 10:12, 11:1, 13, 22; 13:3; 19:9; 30:6 1). We show God our love to Him by hearing and obeying His Word, and by sharing it with others. If we love God like we say we do, His truth will be a part of our normal daily conversation. We also show our love to God by appreciating His blessings. Love the Lord with all your heart!

Deuteronomy 6:10-15 cautions or warns against disobedience because times of prosperity become times of temptation, if we receive the gifts but fail to thank the Giver. God is our giver of all good gifts; meditate on it, but don't forget or fail to thank God. Please take a look at Deuteronomy 6:10-15:

> *"¹⁰When the LORD your God brings you into the land he swore to your fathers, to Abraham, Isaac and Jacob, to give you-a land with large, flourishing cities you did not build, ¹¹houses filled with all kinds of good things you did not provide, wells you did not dig, and vineyards and olive groves you did not plant-then when you eat and are satisfied, ¹²be careful that you do not forget the LORD, who brought you out of Egypt, out of the land of slavery. ¹³Fear the LORD your God, serve him only and take your oaths in his name. ¹⁴Do not follow other gods, the gods of the peoples around you; "¹⁵for the LORD your God, who is among you, is a jealous God and his anger will burn against you, and he will destroy you from the face of the land."*

_____

_____

_____

_____

When you really understand how good God is to you; you will have no interest in the temptations the enemy puts before you. When you are tempted, count your blessings; and you will soon have strength to say NO. Every good and perfect gift is from above, coming down from the Father of the heavenly lights, who does not change like shifting shadows (James 1:17). Being aware of God's love for you can make you a stronger, better and more confident person.

Love the Lord your God with all your heart, all your soul, and all your strength." Because God cannot accept half-hearted worship or half-hearted OBEDIENCE:

> *"Not with eyeservice, as men pleasers; but as the servants of Christ, doing the will of God from the heart;"* Ephesians 6:6 (KJV).

I looked up "half-hearted" in the English dictionary and found, the adjective HALF-HEARTED has one sense:

> *1. feeling or showing little interest or enthusiasm*

As I stated earlier, God cannot and will not accept half-hearted worship or half-hearted OBEDIENCE. God is calling out to his lukewarm (half-hearted) people. God is calling out to his half-hearted people to turn from their idolatry, their spiritual adultery, and their lukewarmness. God wants them to get on fire for the Lord and for His Word, and for faithfulness and obedience to Him...

In conclusion, show God, you really love Him! Anything you do; if you do it to bring glory to God, and do it with the love of Jesus Christ, this shows God, you really love him! As long as you do it with your heart, a heart that loves God. We cannot fool God; He knows and sees everything! In other words, we cannot fool God or hide from Him. Nothing is hidden from God (Hebrews 4:13).

NOTES:

www.ingramcontent.com/pod-product-compliance
Lightning Source LLC
LaVergne TN
LVHW041545070526
838199LV00046B/1839